D0015726

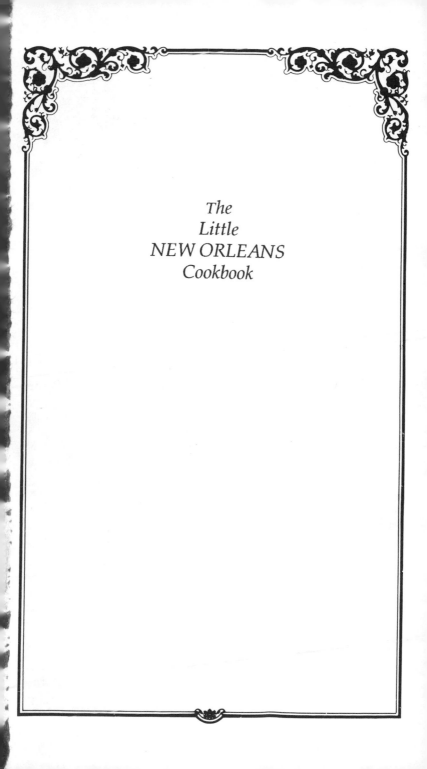

The
Little
NEW ORLEANS
Cookbook

St. Louis Cathedral, in the heart of the French Quarter.

The
Little
NEW ORLEANS
Cookbook

◆

**FIFTY-SEVEN
CLASSIC CREOLE RECIPES
THAT WILL
ENABLE EVERYONE
TO ENJOY
THE SPECIAL
CUISINE
OF
NEW ORLEANS**

by

Gwen McKee

Illustrations by Joseph A. Arrigo

QUAIL RIDGE PRESS
Baton Rouge/Brandon

DEDICATION

**To my dear little mother,
Esther Grace McLin,
whose prayers
are always with us,
and who delights us with her
wonderful tales and tastes of
New Orleans.**

Copyright © 1991 by
Quail Ridge Press
www.quailridge.com
ISBN 0-937552-42-9

Photos courtesy Louisiana Office of Tourism
and by Gwen McKee

First printing, November 1991 • Second, October 1993
Third, February 1995 • Fourth, August 1998 • Fifth, January 2001
Sixth, January 2003 • Seventh, November 2002

Printed in Canada

Library of Congress Cataloging-in-Publication Data

McKee, Gwen.
    The Little New Orleans cookbook / by Gwen McKee:
drawings by Joe Arrigo.
        p. cm.
    Includes index.
    ISBN 0-937552-42-9: $8.95
    1. Cookery, American--Louisiana style. 2. Cookery--
Louisiana--New Orleans. I. Title.
TX715.2.L68M37 1991
641.59763'35--dc20   91-24631
                                    CIP

CONTENTS

CONTENTS

CONTENTS

Artists on the square in front of the historic Cabildo.

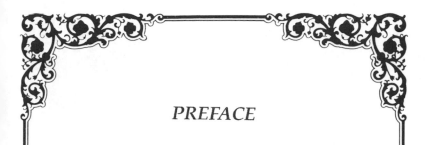

PREFACE

New Orleans *is* good food. Ask anyone who has visited the city how their trip was and they will always begin with, "I've never had such delicious food!" And they will search for superlatives to try to describe it—which is virtually impossible. The cuisine of New Orleans literally defies description.

Most people tend to think they must return to the Crescent City to enjoy the kind of wonderful dining they experienced there. Well, it ain't necessarily so! It is most *definitely* attainable.

Within these pages are some of the classic recipes of New Orleans presented in a clear, easy-to-follow style. Cooking should be fun, so I have added some light-hearted notes with helpful hints tucked within. It is a fact that in Louisiana, food is more than a necessity of life, it is a *way* of life. Few would argue that putting fun into food is probably the underlying "secret ingredient" to all good Cajun and Creole cuisine.

Many of the now world-famous New Orleans dishes originated in the restaurants. Embellishing on the unique Creole style and flavor, these talented chefs have flambéed, soufléed, blackened, frothed, sauced, and presented their creations with such pride and flair that their customers always go away feeling they have had more than a meal...they have had a memorable experience.

What most visitors don't get to experience is the wonderful home cookin' of New Orleans. It was in the home kitchens that the French, Spanish, African, and Indian influences all blended together to give birth to Creole cooking. The étouffées and gumbos and bread puddings you may have enjoyed at a particular New Orleans eatery more than likely had their origins in home kitchens. They were usually created out of necessity by using whatever was plentiful at the market, available from the vegetable wagon, or left in the cupboard. Whether it was ripe bananas, leftover rice, stale bread...these home cooks found a way to put foods together deliciously!

I have coupled the recipes and stories of my many New Orleans ancestors with my own research to bring you these typical Creole recipes, making them as easy to prepare and up-to-date as I can, so that you will not be afraid to incorporate them into your everyday cooking. I cannot resist giving my own personal tidbits—and I take that author's privilege to embellish, take out a few calories, simplify, or whatever it takes to encourage you to try them.

Working on this book has been one of the most enjoyable projects I have ever undertaken. I would literally lose all track of time going back to the many cherished moments in my life that have revolved around the enjoyment of good food. I wish to thank my mother for recollecting her recipes (and delightful stories that go with them); and Lois for sharing her intuitive methods with Creole cooking; and Barney and Barbara and Sheila for all their help and patience throughout the making of this book. I particularly

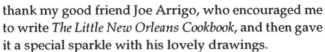

thank my good friend Joe Arrigo, who encouraged me to write *The Little New Orleans Cookbook*, and then gave it a special sparkle with his lovely drawings.

I truly believe the best eating in the world can be found in New Orleans. My hope is that some of the heritage and enthusiasm and enjoyment that have long been embroidered through this wonderful Creole cuisine will spill out of these pages into your own kitchen. The taste of the Crescent City is right here in your hands. I warmly extend my invitation in that charmingly unique New Orleans dialect...

"Welcome to Dahlishous N'Awlins, Dawlin!"

Gwen McKee

The music of the street musicians can be heard throughout the Quarter.

N'AWLINS SEASONING

Shake New Orleans flavor into all your Creole cookin'!

1 tablespoon garlic powder
1 tablespoon onion powder
2 tablespoons thyme
2 tablespoons crushed bay leaves
1 tablespoon parsley flakes
1 teaspoon basil leaves
2 tablespoons black pepper
1 tablespoon cayenne pepper
1 teaspoon Accent (optional)
1 cup salt (or Lite Salt)

Mix all together in a quart jar, cover tightly and shake. Fill shakers (the ones with dial tops and large holes are perfect) or spice jars.

NOTE: I cannot recommend highly enough that you make this for all your Creole and Cajun cooking. I call for it in a number of recipes in this book. You can substitute bought Creole seasonings, but this one is specifically *N'Awlins*! It can be used in recipes calling for a combination of salt and seasonings—saves lots of time measuring it all out. Fill shakers or spice jars and give to your friends with a ribbon tied around—they will thank you every time they use it.

FRENCH BREAD
The Bread of New Orleans

So much a part of New Orleans cuisine is this all-important bread that it deserves its own special place in a New Orleans cookbook—but I do not give a recipe because I have rarely made it. Nobody makes it—my grandmothers didn't even make it. What they did, however, was make things with it: garlic bread, po-boys, bread puddings, French toast, all kinds of stuffings and dressings—nary a crumb is wasted. It's such a necessary part of the enjoyment of gumbo and étouffée and jambalaya and on and on and on. My favorite recipe is—go to the bakery and buy it!

NOTE: Bakeries in New Orleans bake a lot more than bread. They are, in fact, incredible places—a feast for the senses. Put cholesterol and diet and all that stuff completely out of your mind before entering one and let your nose lead the way. Petits Fours, Brioche, Strawberry Shortcakes, Neopolitan Squares, Cream Puffs, Wine Cakes, Pecan Pies, Rum Balls, Éclairs, Dobache Cakes—you don't have to know the name... just point to it and say, "I want one of those," and go ahead and indulge, because if any of these things kills you... well, you've already had a little heaven right here on earth!

TOASTY GARLIC ROUNDS

Cut stale French bread into 1/4 - inch rounds; brush one side with olive oil and finely minced garlic. Toast under broiler till light brown.

FRENCHIES
Lusty crusty munchies.

1 (6-roll) package French mini-loaves
1 1/4 sticks butter or margarine
1 teaspoon garlic powder
1 teaspoon Tabasco
1 teaspoon water
1 tablespoon parsley flakes (optional)

Slice French bread into thin rounds (a generous 1/4 inch). Melt margarine; add remaining ingredients. Brush both sides of bread rounds very lightly with butter mixture. Bake on 2 cookie sheets in 225° oven 40 - 50 minutes till dry, but not brown. Turn heat off and leave in oven 30 minutes or more (or overnight). Store in tin or cookie jar.

NOTE: If you freeze the bread first and use a knife with a serrated edge (or an electric knife), it will slice much easier and neater. I make these all the time. They go with almost any meal, are excellent with dips, and break nicely into tasty salad croutons. My friend Eve makes these to take on golf trips—great travel snacks. Better make plenty.

JAZZED-UP FRENCH BREAD

1 loaf French bread
2-3 tablespoons Parmesan cheese
6 ounces soft margarine
2 tablespoons vegetable or olive oil
1 tablespoon water
1/2 teaspoon garlic powder (or more)

Split loaf lengthwise and place cut side up on baking sheet. Sprinkle lightly with Parmesan cheese. Melt margarine with oil, water, and garlic powder; stir. Spoon over loaves evenly. Bake in preheated 400° oven about 20 minutes till crisp and lightly browned.

CAFÉ AU LAIT
(kah-fay oh-lay)

At some time in your French Quarter wanderings, you always find your way to the coffee shops for that special coffee of New Orleans—Café au Lait. You can almost re-create that special Vieux Carré atmosphere by brewing some right in your own kitchen.

Coffee and chicory (or dark roast coffee)
Hot whole milk
Sugar or sweetener (optional)

Heat milk or cream and beat with rotary beater till foamy. Pour equal amounts of coffee and milk into cup at same time. Sweeten to taste.

NOTE: Keeping milk was a problem in the steamy summers of old New Orleans, especially since the ice-man only came once a day. So my grandma kept condensed milk in a jar on the table. They put a spoon of it into their coffee—and they had milk and sugar at the same time! It was also an after school treat to put a heaping spoon of it into the heel of the French bread when it was hot from the bakery. Try it—it's quite good!

The Café Du Monde near the River.

NEW ORLEANS
FRENCH DRIP COFFEE

Dark roast coffee (drip grind)
Boiling water
A French drip coffee pot
A shallow pan
Cream and sugar, if desired

Set coffee pot into shallow pan on burner. Pour boiling water slowly over coffee grounds (about 1 cup water to 2 tablespoons grounds). Pour another cup of boiling water into shallow pan under coffee pot and put on simmer to keep warm.

NOTE: I can still see my grandmother's little white porcelain pot wobbling gently in the simmering water of that tattered tin pan, bent so out of shape by years of use that it never set quite level on the stove. It served many more cups of coffee than it seemed possible for that little pot to hold—of course you never poured more than half a cup. It was sipped... and savored.

BEIGNETS
(ben-yays)

These wonderfully light and puffy donut-type delicacies are served with and often dunked in café au lait.

1 cup whole milk
2 tablespoons shortening (or lard, margarine, or oil)
2 tablespoons sugar
1 (1/4-ounce) package dry yeast
3 cups plain flour
1 teaspoon salt
1 egg
Oil for deep frying
Powdered sugar

Heat milk till almost boiling, stirring so as not to scorch. Place shortening and sugar in a big bowl; pour scalded milk over and stir until smooth and melted. Cool to lukewarm, then add yeast; stir till dissolved.

Sift dry flour and salt into another bowl. Stir about half of this flour mixture into the milk mixture gradually, then add egg. Beat batter thoroughly, stirring in remaining flour a little at a time. Cover with a towel and set aside for about an hour till it doubles in bulk. Knead gently on floured board; roll to 1/4-inch thickness. Cut into 2-inch squares (or diamonds) with a sharp knife. Cover and let rise again 30-45 minutes.

Drop squares into hot oil (385°), turning once when golden brown on bottom side. Drain on paper towels and dust with sifted powdered sugar. Serve warm. Makes about 2 dozen.

NOTE: Beignet mixes are widely available and require only that you add water, then mix and fry—they're quite good. Or make **Mock Beignets:** Cut flattened canned biscuits in half and fry in hot oil till golden on each side, then dust in powdered sugar.

CALAS
(cah-lays)

In old New Orleans, the street vendors carried these fried rice balls in baskets on their heads, calling, "Belle cala! Tout chaud!"

1 1/2 cups cooked rice
1 1/2 cups flour
1 1/2 teaspoons baking powder
1/4 teaspoon salt
1/8 teaspoon nutmeg
3 eggs, beaten
2 tablespoons milk
1 teaspoon vanilla
Cooking oil
Powdered sugar

Mix rice with dry ingredients. Add eggs, milk, and vanilla, and mix well. Shape into 2-inch balls (or drop by tablespoonfuls) into hot deep fat and fry until brown. Drain on paper towels. Sprinkle with powdered sugar. Makes about 12 balls.

NOTE: The Creole cooks never wasted anything. After dinner, they mixed a cake of yeast with a little water and the leftover rice. The next morning they mixed in the other ingredients (minus the baking powder), fried them, and served them with their café au lait. The baking powder recipe is a little easier, but the yeast makes them awfully good. Some restaurants still offer these tasty French-fried goodies.

PAIN PERDU

(pahn pear-doo')

Also referred to as French Toast, pain perdu literally means "lost bread" as it is made from very stale bread that's about to be "lost." What a rejuvenation!

2 tablespoons butter
2 tablespoons oil
2 eggs, well beaten
1 cup milk
2 tablespoons sugar
Pinch salt
1/2 teaspoon vanilla
1/2 teaspoon cinnamon mixed with
2 teaspoons sugar (optional)
8 - 10 slices stale French bread (about 1 inch thick)

Heat butter and oil in large skillet. Mix eggs, milk, sugar, salt, and vanilla in large deep bowl. Soak bread slices by wiggling the bowl till all slices are coated, then let sit till bread soaks up all liquid. (Or cover and let soak all night in refrigerator). Place slices in skillet and sprinkle with cinnamon/sugar mixture. Turn to brown moderately on each side. Sprinkle with powdered sugar, or serve with cane syrup. Serves 3 - 5.

Low-cal / Low-cholesterol: Use egg substitute (like Scramblers or Egg Beaters), or 2 eggs with one of the yolks thrown out. Use skim milk, sugar sweetener, and low-fat margarine or vegetable cooking spray. Good to substitute pineapple or orange juice for the milk. Any kind of sliced bread is good—I like wheat—and if it isn't stale, encourage it to be so by putting it in the toaster till hot, but not toasted, and leaving it on the counter for awhile.

GRILLADES AND GRITS
(gree'-yads)

Traditionally a hearty breakfast dish, this is delicious any-time! Perfect for a New Orleans Jazz Brunch. Rice, pasta, toast are good understudies for the grits.

2 pounds veal or beef round, about 1/2-inch thick
Salt and pepper
2 tablespoons flour
2 tablespoons vegetable oil
2 tablespoons butter
1 cup chopped onion
1/2 cup chopped celery
1/2 cup chopped green pepper
1 (16-ounce) can tomatoes
1 tablespoon chopped parsley
1 cup water
1/4 teaspoon thyme
1/2 teaspoon Tabasco sauce

Pound trimmed veal with mallet or edge of plate. Sprinkle with salt, pepper, and flour on both sides. Cut into 2-inch squares and fry in oil and butter in deep skillet till brown. Remove meat to a platter and brown remaining flour in skillet. (You just made a roux!) Add onion, celery, and green pepper and cook till soft.

Return meat to pan and add tomatoes, parsley, water (good to use part red wine), and remaining seasonings. Bring to a boil, stir, cover and simmer about an hour. Serve over hot buttered grits. Serves about 6.

NOTE: Grits are very New Orleans. But they have to be cooked properly. Gritty grits that sit up high like mashed potatoes turn a lot of first-timers off. Creamy grits that fall off the spoon easily and lay down almost flatly on the plate get a high degree of come-back-for more folks. Try some of these popular variations.

MICRO-GRITS: In an 8-cup measure, bring 3 cups water and 1/2 teaspoon salt to a boil in micro on HIGH (takes about 4 - 5 minutes); add 7/8 cup grits, stir and cover. Micro on #7 for 3 1/2 minutes. Stir and let sit another 2 minutes. Creamy and perfect!

CHEESE GRITS: To 4 cups cooked grits, add a beaten egg, a roll of garlic (or jalapeño or sharp) cheese, 1 teaspoon Worcestershire, few dashes Tabasco, 6 table-spoons butter—bake a half hour or so in a moderate oven. Wonderful!

JAMBALAYA GRITS: Make a roux with bacon grease and flour, then sauté chopped onion, bell pepper, cel-ery, garlic; add cooked grits, tomatoes, and ham; crumble some cooked bacon on top. The proportions are varied—make up your own. *Very* Louisiana—after all, the Holy Trinity has blessed yet another dish!

NOTE: So revered and imperative to Creole and Cajun cooking are onion, bell pepper and celery, that they are affectionately referred to as "the Holy Trinity."

DAUBE GLACÉ
(dohb glah-say)

Next time you have roast beef, put a few slices aside and try this outstanding do-ahead appetizer—impresses your guests, especially the men.

10 stuffed olives, sliced
2 cans beef consommé
4 ribs celery, minced
1 bunch green onions, minced
1 clove garlic, finely minced (optional)
1 carrot, chopped finely
6 tablespoons parsley flakes
2 tablespoons Worcestershire sauce
1/8 teaspoon Cayenne pepper
2 tablespoons unflavored gelatin
1/4 cup cold water
1 cup shredded cooked beef

Arrange olives in bottom of loaf pan. In a saucepan, bring remaining ingredients to a boil except gelatin, water, and beef; simmer about 10 minutes. Dissolve gelatin in water; add to consommé and stir to dissolve. Add meat and stir. Pour into pan and refrigerate several hours till set. Serve with Ritz or other crackers.

NOTE: This is also done with beef shinbones and pigs feet and stuff that jellies itself—I'm grateful to whoever put gelatin in a box.

AUNT LOU'S CRABMEAT MORNAY

A delicious tradition.

**1 stick real butter
1 bunch green onions, chopped
1/2 bunch parsley, finely chopped
2 tablespoons flour
1 (16-ounce) carton Half and Half
1/2 pound sliced Swiss cheese
1 tablespoon sherry wine
1/8 teaspoon cayenne pepper
1/4 teaspoon salt
1 pound lump crabmeat**

Melt butter in heavy pot on medium heat. Sauté chopped onions in butter till soft. Add parsley. Stir in flour, then cream, then cheese, and stir gently till cheese is melted. Add sherry and seasonings, then fold in picked crabmeat. Heat only till thickened; do not boil. Serve in chafing dish over low heat with *Frenchies* or Melba rounds for dipping. Also superb in patty shells.

NOTE: There has never been a family Christmas party without *Aunt Lou's Crabmeat Mornay.* She makes two separate batches early in the day and refrigerates them till party time, heating one batch at a time on the stovetop before taking it to its revered place at the dining room table. Understandably, there's always a crowd at that end of the table. Those who are scraping the last available smidgeon from the bottom of the dish literally cheer when the second batch arrives!

SEAFOOD GUMBO

I overheard some very serious Cajuns bragging that gumbo is "The National Dish of Louisiana"—never have figured that one out. But I know for sure it's the state dish—and well it should be. Mon cher, c'est magnifique!

1/2 cup vegetable oil
1/2 cup flour
2 large onions, chopped
3 - 4 stalks celery, chopped
1 bell pepper, chopped (optional)
1 clove garlic, minced
1 (8-ounce) can tomato sauce
1 (1-pound) can tomatoes, chopped
2 cups stock (seafood, chicken, or canned chicken broth)
1 quart water
2 (10-ounce) boxes frozen cut okra
1 teaspoon each: Salt, crushed bay leaves, thyme
1/2 teaspoon cayenne pepper
2 - 3 pounds raw peeled seafood (shrimp,
crawfish tails, crabmeat, mild fish)
Filé (optional)

Brown flour in oil in large heavy pot slowly, stirring to make mahogany brown roux. Add chopped vegetables and sauté till soft. Add tomato sauce and tomatoes, chicken stock, water, okra, and seasonings. Stir and simmer about 45 minutes. Add seafood of choice and cook another 20-30 minutes. Serve around a scoop of hot rice in a soup dish. Offer filé (ground sassafras leaves) at table, if you like. Serves 8 - 10.

NOTE: I have such a passion for gumbo that I wrote a book on it! *The Little Gumbo Book* stresses making gumbo the day before you want to serve it. Refrigerate overnight, or freeze for later. These wonderful flavors like time to "marry."

Narrow passageways open onto graceful courtyards.
The Gumbo Shop.

COURTBOUILLON

(coo'-bee-yohn)

A fancy fish stew that's sure to please.

1/2 cup vegetable oil
2 large onions, chopped
3 ribs celery, chopped
1/2 bell pepper, chopped
1 bunch green onions, chopped
2 cloves garlic, minced
3 teaspoons *N'Awlins Seasoning*
2 (16-ounce) cans tomatoes
1 quart fish stock or water
6 slices redfish or red snapper (about 3 pounds)
4 thin lemon slices
1 cup dry red wine

In large heavy pot, sauté chopped vegetables in oil till soft. Stir in seasoning and tomatoes and simmer for 10 minutes. Add stock and cook slowly 30 minutes. Then add fish and simmer another 30 minutes. Lastly add lemon slices and wine, bring to boil, and serve. Serves 8.

NOTE: Try making your own stock: If you can't catch one, go to the seafood market and get a whole fish, clean and fillet it, then boil the bones, skin, and head with some Creole seasoning, a celery stalk or two and a couple of onion quarters, and let it simmer an hour or more. Strain it and save that wonderful fish stock. There's a lot of flavor in dem dare bones! (Your cat will be sorely disappointed in this procedure.)

CRAB AND CORN BISQUE

1/2 pound butter
3 tablespoons flour
1 large onion, chopped
1 quart milk
1 (16-ounce) can cream style corn
1 can cream of potato soup
1/4 teaspoon mace
1/4 teaspoon red pepper
1 pint picked crabmeat
1/4 pound grated Swiss cheese
2 tablespoons snipped parsley
2 tablespoons finely chopped green onions

In large heavy pot, melt butter. Stir in flour till well blended, but not brown; add onions. Cook on medium heat till onions are soft—about 10 minutes. Add all but last four ingredients. Simmer about 15 minutes—be careful not to scorch. Before serving, stir in crabmeat, cheese, parsley and green onions. Serves 6 - 8 elegantly.

NOTE: This is to die for! Take a taste, close your eyes, and you very well may hear "dah saints go marchin' in."

Courtyards are favorite places for dining.
Court of Two Sisters.

OYSTER STEW

New Orleanians often serve this as the soup du jour.

1/2 cup butter or margarine
3 tablespoons flour
6 - 8 green onions, finely chopped
2 stalks celery, finely chopped
2 (12-ounce) jars oysters
1 quart milk, heated, but not boiled
1 teaspoon Creole seasoning
1/2 teaspoon minced garlic
1 teaspoon Tabasco
Croutons or oyster crackers
Snipped parsley

Over medium-low heat, melt butter in big, heavy pot. Stir in flour only till blended. Add onions and celery and sauté slowly till soft. Add oyster liquid and blend well. Now add milk, then oysters (cut in half if they are big) and seasonings. Simmer gently for 10-15 minutes, being careful not to let it get to a heavy boil. When oysters begin to curl, it is ready to serve. Ladle into bowls with croutons (or broken *Frenchies*) and fresh parsley sprinkled on top. Beautiful! Serves 8.

NOTE: This is so incredibly good that your guests will come back for seconds—you may want it to be the main course!

PERFECT BOILED SHRIMP

No guesswork—perfect every time.

1 onion, peeled and quartered
2 cloves garlic
2 tablespoons vegetable oil
1/2 lemon, sliced
1 tablespoon vinegar
1/2 teaspoon Tabasco
1/2 teaspoon black pepper
2 pounds unpeeled headless shrimp
2 teaspoons liquid crab boil (or 1 seasoning bag)
3 tablespoons salt

Fill a 5-quart pot half full of water; bring to a boil. Add all but shrimp, crab boil and salt; return to a boil and add shrimp and crab boil. Boil 5 minutes, then stir in salt to dissolve. Cover, remove from heat, and let set 30 minutes. Remove drained shrimp to a large bowl and cover with ice. Serve right away or chilled.

NOTE: If you can't get crab boil, do without. Spread out the newspaper and bring on the sauce! I promise when you serve these boiled shrimp, you will surely "pass a good time."

LAFITTE'S BLACKSMITH SHOP, NEW ORLEANS

PASSION COCKTAIL SAUCE

Not to be confused with ho-hum sauce, this one will make your nose tingle!

1 cup ketchup
1 tablespoon lemon juice
4 tablespoons horseradish
1/2 teaspoon Tabasco
1 teaspoon Worcestershire sauce
1/4 teaspoon onion powder

Mix and store in a jar in the refrigerator.

NOTE: Superb with boiled shrimp and crawfish, and perfect for raw oysters.

I was just a little girl when my daddy brought home a sack of oysters. He opened one and I thought the shell was very pretty. The oyster, however, didn't look like something I'd want to eat! I watched my daddy slide it off the shell into his mouth, and his facial expression said that it was some kind of good! He opened one and offered it to me. I trusted my daddy explicitly, so I cautiously accepted it. Didn't go down very gracefully, as I recall, but it pleased my daddy so much that I took another. And another. We made up this sauce, and before long I was anxiously waiting for him to pry those shells open! That was a very special night—I became a full-fledged raw oyster lover, and my daddy and I developed a very special bond. (My mother checked on me all night to be sure I was still breathing.)

BIG EASY
BARBECUED SHRIMP

Not to be confused with the outdoor-on-the-grill kind, these shrimp are baked and served in a peppery lemon-butter sauce with hot French bread for soppin'. Mmmmmm...Yeah!

2 pounds large shrimp in shells
1 cup butter
Juice of 2 lemons
2 tablespoons minced garlic
1 teaspoon N'Awlins Seasoning
2 tablespoons Worcestershire or soy sauce
2 tablespoons black pepper

Wash shrimp well and drain in colander, then lay them in a large baking pan. Heat remaining ingredients except pepper in saucepan 2-3 minutes; pour over shrimp. Sprinkle generously with black pepper. Put the squeezed lemon halves on top. Bake in 375° oven 15-20 minutes. Serve unpeeled with sauce along with lots of hot French bread for dunking. Incredible! Serves 6.

NOTE: This is what you'll likely get if you order barbecued shrimp in New Orleans... and you'll be glad you did. Get some big napkins and try it yourself.

REMOULADE SAUCE

(raw-mo-lawd)

A cool New Orleans classic.

**3 minced green onions
2 ribs celery, minced
1/2 cup minced parsley
3 tablespoons minced dill pickle
1 3/4 cups vegetable oil
2/3 cup Creole mustard (or prepared)
2 tablespoons horseradish
3 tablespoons lemon juice
1 tablespoon paprika
1/2 teaspoon salt
1/2 teaspoon sugar**

It's important that everything is minced finely. Put all ingredients in a quart jar, mix well, and refrigerate. Keeps for several weeks and makes enough for about 8 - 10 servings.

For individual servings, spoon 2 - 3 tablespoons chilled sauce over 1/2 cup cold boiled shrimp on a bed of shredded lettuce. Pretty (and delicious) arranged with tomato and boiled egg wedges.

NOTE: Mostly identified with shrimp, this is superb with lobster or crabmeat or fish. It's also excellent over lettuce wedges, tomatoes, avocados... ice cream (just kidding).

MICRO-ROUX

Start with a roux, end with a masterpiece! A microwave roux with the veggies cooked in—so easy you may never do it any other way!

2/3 cup vegetable oil
2/3 cup flour
2/3 cup chopped onions
2/3 cup chopped green pepper
2/3 cup chopped celery
2/3 cup chopped green onions
2/3 teaspoon minced garlic
2/3 cup water

Mix oil with flour in a 4-cup glass measuring bowl. Microwave uncovered on HIGH for 6 minutes. Stir and cook another 30-60 seconds on HIGH till the color of mahogany.

Now add chopped vegetables, stir well, and "sauté" them on HIGH for another 5 minutes, till soft but not brown. Before stirring, pour oil off top. Add hot tap water and stir till smooth. So easy, freezable... and just right!

NOTE: A roux is simply a mixture of flour and fat cooked and stirred till it is brown. The browning takes away the raw pasty taste of white flour and gives it a nut-like, roasted flavor that is so wonderfully Creole.

DRY ROUX

Put several cups of flour in a large heavy pot and brown at 400° for about an hour, being sure to stir every 15 minutes or so. Or do it on top the stove, stirring constantly about 15 minutes. Store in jar in cabinet. Mix equal parts dry roux and water (or oil), stirring till smooth. Add to gumbos, soups, stews, gravies. Get the taste without the calories!

SHRIMP CREOLE

So very New Orleans... simple to prepare, elegant to serve, and extremely pleasurable to eat!

1 recipe *Micro-roux*
1 (6-ounce) can tomato paste
1 (8-ounce) can tomato sauce
1 cup water
1/2 teaspoon each: Thyme, crushed bay leaves, salt
1/8 teaspoon cayenne pepper
1 1/2 pounds peeled raw shrimp

Pour *Micro-roux* into heavy pot over medium heat. Add remaining ingredients except shrimp. Bring to boil, then add shrimp and simmer about 10 minutes uncovered; stir, cover, turn off heat, and let sit about 15 minutes or more. Serve over hot fluffy rice (serves 6) with *Jazzed-Up French Bread*, steamed broccoli and *Sensation Salad*.

NOTE: One of the joys of having *N'Awlins Seasoning* (page 13) is that you can substitute 1 1/2 teaspoons in place of all the seasonings mentioned above. Also do try to get fresh shrimp—they are prettier, have a better texture and, well, they just seem to stay perkier longer with their good flavor still tucked inside their shells.

CRAWFISH ÉTOUFFÉE
(craw-fish aye-too-faye)

Also spelled crayfish, the local pronunciation is most decidedly crawfish... or crawdad... or mudbug....

1 stick butter
3 ribs celery, chopped
3 onions, chopped
1 bell pepper, chopped
3 cloves garlic, minced
3 tablespoons flour
2 pounds crawfish tails
1 1/2 cups water
2 tablespoons tomato paste (no more)
1 tablespoon lemon juice
1/2 teaspoon salt
1/8 teaspoon cayenne pepper
1/2 teaspoon basil
1/2 teaspoon thyme
1/4 teaspoon chili powder
1/4 teaspoon ground cloves
2 tablespoons minced parsley
3 - 4 chopped green onions

Melt butter in large, heavy skillet. Add celery, onions, bell pepper and garlic and sauté on medium heat till soft. Stir in flour. Add crawfish tails, water, tomato paste, lemon juice, and seasonings. Stir and cook about 15 minutes. Cover and simmer another 15 minutes. Stir in parsley and green onions, re-cover, and remove from heat. Serve over hot fluffy rice. Serves 8.

NOTE: Fresh or frozen shrimp substitutes deliciously! Absolutely incredible taste! I recently discovered this makes an attention-getting dip when I needed an hors d'oeuvre to take to an impromptu neighborhood gathering. Had some étouffée leftover from the previous night's dinner party, so I brought some with a basket of *Frenchies*—what a hit! Another amazing "make-do."

Jackson Square is a magnet for artists, performers, and visitors.

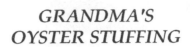

GRANDMA'S
OYSTER STUFFING

1 big onion, chopped
2 ribs celery, chopped
1 large pod garlic, minced
1/2 stick butter or margarine
1 (12-ounce) jar oysters, reserve liquid
2 tablespoons chopped parsley
4 ounces stale French bread (1/4 loaf)
4 ounces herb seasoned stuffing mix
1/2 teaspoon salt
1/2 teaspoon black pepper
1/8 teaspoon cayenne

Sauté onion, celery, and garlic in butter in large heavy skillet or pot till soft. Add oysters (cut if big) and parsley and cook until edges of oysters curl. Soak stale French bread in a bowl of ice water, then squeeze most of water out. Add squeezed bread, stuffing mix, 1/2 cup oyster liquor (use cream if you don't have enough), and remaining ingredients to pot. Stir and cook over low heat about 15 minutes. Loosely stuff chicken or turkey, or bake separately in greased baking dish at 350° about 30 minutes. Serves 6.

NOTE: Going to Grandma's was always a treat. It never dawned on me that she was poor, because she had things like jelly donuts and French fries and fried chicken... and always a ready nickel for a flavored "sno-ball" down the street. Her little kitchen brimmed with her goodies and her warmth and her love. She left us some treasured memories... and delicious recipes. Now that I think about it, she was just as rich as I thought she was.

OYSTERS ROCKEFELLER

Jules Alciatore, son of the founder of Antoine's, created a secret green sauce for oysters, and gave it the richest name he could think of. This is a splendid rendition.

3 dozen fresh oysters
1 bunch fresh spinach
1 bunch fresh parsley
1 bunch fresh green onions
Leaves from 1/2 bunch fresh celery
1/4 head fresh lettuce
1/2 cup butter, softened
3/4 cup bread crumbs
1 teaspoon anchovy paste
1 ounce absinthe (optional)
1/8 teaspoon Tabasco
1 tablespoon Worcestershire
1/4 cup grated Parmesan cheese
Rock salt*

Drain oysters well, saving juice. Mince all greens finely in food processor or blender. Mix butter and 1/4 cup bread crumbs in large bowl; add greens and mix, adding oyster liquor if needed to make of spreading consistency. Add remaining ingredients except Parmesan and remaining bread crumbs. Mix well.

Place rock salt in baking or pie pans and heat about 20 minutes in 450° oven. Place cleaned half shells on rock salt, place oysters back in shells, and spread 2 tablespoons of green sauce over each. Combine Parmesan and remaining bread crumbs and sprinkle a teaspoon on each oyster. Bake at 400° about 20 minutes till lightly browned. Serves 6.

NOTE: *Rock salt keeps the oysters level and hot, and it looks pretty, but they bake just as well on a naked pan. This can be served as an appetizer or the entrée. Worth every bit of the effort... and agreeably, as rich as Rockefeller.

TROUT AMANDINE

Of the many famous New Orleans ways to cook these lovely speckled beauties, this is perhaps the most requested—and certainly easy to prepare.

6 speckled trout
Cold milk
Seasoned flour
1 3/4 sticks butter
1 cup (or more) slivered almonds
2 tablespoons chopped parsley
2 tablespoons fresh lemon juice
Salt and pepper

Skin and fillet trout; soak in cold milk for 10 minutes or so, then drain. Roll in seasoned flour; shake off excess. Fry in 1 stick melted butter in heavy frying pan a few at a time, only long enough to just cook—a few minutes on each side until golden and crisp. Keep warm on heated platter.

In same skillet, melt remaining butter, and lightly brown almonds; add parsley, lemon juice, salt and pepper. Simmer a few minutes, then pour sauce over crispy fish. Serves 6.

NOTE: My daddy often went to a fishing camp for the weekend, so we always had fish. They were usually mealed and fried quickly in hot shortening in a big iron skillet. Grease popped everywhere (much to my mother's chagrin), but the come-on-in smell seemed to assure company even if you weren't expecting any—a good time was gah-rohn-teed!

TARTAR SAUCE

1 cup mayonnaise or salad dressing
1/2 cup chopped dill pickle
1 tablespoon minced onion
2 tablespoons chopped parsley
1 teaspoon Tabasco
1 teaspoon lemon juice

Mix and refrigerate.

NOTE: New Orleans is a city of water-water-every-where, and has such an abundance of fresh fish and seafood that tartar sauce is a staple just like mayonnaise and Tabasco.

The Creole Queen *on the Mississippi River.*

BLACKENED REDFISH

4 redfish fillets (or other firm fish)
Seasoning Mix
1 stick butter, melted

Dry fish and refrigerate; prepare *Seasoning Mix*.

Use only a black iron Dutch oven or skillet because that's the only thing that can take the heat. Place it perfectly empty on high heat.

Lay fillets on waxed paper and sprinkle lightly with seasoning mix, then dip in melted butter. When the Dutch oven is so hot that it has a white circle in the bottom, immediately drop fish in and stand back—it will sizzle and spatter and smoke. Turn fillet after about 30-40 seconds and blacken the other side another 30-40 seconds; remove to serving plates. Better to do only 1 or 2 at a time. Repeat for other fillets. Remove Dutch oven from heat. Serves 4.

SEASONING MIX
2 teaspoons paprika
2 tablespoons crushed bay leaves
1/2 teaspoon granulated onion
1/2 teaspoon granulated garlic
1/4 teaspoon basil
1/4 teaspoon oregano
1/4 teaspoon thyme
3 teaspoons salt
1/4 teaspoon black pepper
1/2 teaspoon white pepper
1/4 teaspoon cayenne pepper

Mix all well in jar. This keeps well and is good on other Creole dishes.

NOTE: The quickest, tastiest fish dish you'll ever cook is this variation of Paul Prudhomme's famous dish. Thanks to him Creole and Cajun cuisine has been elevated to new heights all over the world. *N'Awlins Seasoning* subs quite well for *Seasoning Mix*.

OYSTER PO-BOYS
(oyee-stah poh-boys)

"A recipe for po-boys? You're kidding! Everybody knows how to make po-boys." Well, just in case...

Oysters (about 1 per inch of bread)
Corn flour, salt, pepper
Po-boy bread or French mini-loaves
Mayonnaise, salad dressing or tartar sauce
Tomato slices
Shredded lettuce
Dill pickle slices (optional)
Salt, pepper to taste

Dip drained oysters in seasoned corn flour and fry quickly in very hot oil; drain on paper towels. Heat French bread in oven just long enough to get hot—do not toast. Split and spread generously with mayonnaise. Cover with hot oysters, tomato slices, lettuce and a few pickles. Put the top half on and give it one good mash with the palm of your hand... and chomp in! Have the ketchup handy... and the Tabasco.

NOTE: Fried shrimp, roast beef and gravy, ham and cheese, softshell crab and crawfish are other popular choices. Be sure to order your po-boy "dressed" if you want to get lettuce and tomatoes. And if you want to make these with any other kind of bread, go ahead, but you'll have to call it something else. It just ain't a real po-boy if you don't have that light-on-the-inside, crusty-on-the-outside New Orleans French bread!

MUFFULETTAS
*(muf-uh-lot-uz)**

*Hard to beat the ones at Central Grocery across from the French Market... but these will almost take you there. *(The Italians there pronounce it "moof-uh-leh-tuh.")*

1 round loaf soft Italian bread
Olive oil
3 slices baked ham
3 slices Provolone cheese
6 slices Genoa-style salami
3 slices Swiss cheese
4 tablespoons *Olive Salad*

Split bread on the round and brush with olive oil. Alternate thin slices of hams and cheeses on one side. Top with *Olive Salad* and replace top. Serves 2-3.

NOTE: Great with any crusty-top roll. Okay to heat briefly just long enough to soften the cheeses.

OLIVE SALAD
1/2 cup pimento-stuffed olives
1 cup black olives
1/2 cup finely chopped celery
1/4 cup finely chopped carrots
1/4 cup finely chopped cauliflower (optional)
1 tablespoon chopped green pepper
1 tablespoon parsley
2 teaspoons minced garlic
1 tablespoon minced onion
1 cup olive oil
1/3 cup vegetable oil
1/2 teaspoon each: Salt, oregano, coarse black pepper

Mix all together in a quart jar. Keeps well refrigerated.

NOTE: New Orleans Italians paint their cuisine right into the whole Creole picture. You can make a quick Wop Salad (which they named themselves) by spooning some of the *Olive Salad* atop crisp salad greens.

CHICKEN FRICASSEE
Creole Smothered Chicken

1 chicken, cut in pieces
2/3 cup flour (salt and pepper added)
1/3 cup vegetable oil
1/4 cup margarine
2 onions, chopped
2 ribs celery, chopped
1 clove garlic, minced
2 3/4 cups water or chicken stock
1 bay leaf
1/2 teaspoon thyme
Dash cayenne pepper
Salt and pepper to taste
2 green onions, chopped
2 tablespoons chopped parsley

Dredge chicken pieces in seasoned flour, and brown slowly in hot oil. Remove chicken. Discard all but 1 tablespoon oil. Add margarine and remaining seasoned flour (about 1/3 cup), cooking slowly while stirring till just lightly browned. Add onions, celery and garlic; sauté till soft, about 5 minutes. Add water or stock and seasonings, stirring well. Return chicken to pot, cover, and simmer slowly till chicken is tender, about 30 minutes. Add a few chopped green onions and parsley, remove bay leaf and cook additional 5 minutes. Serve over rice. Serves 6.

CHICKEN SAUCE PIQUANT: Sauté a chopped green pepper with the other vegetables—throw in a can each of stewed tomatoes and tomato sauce, and add a smidgeon more cayenne.

NOTE: Creole dishes don't have to be overly hot—the word is *spicy*. Specifically, I use 1/8 teaspoon each of black and red pepper in this recipe, but start with dashes—you can always *add* pepper.

PANÉED VEAL CUTLETS
(pah-nayd)

The aroma of this cooking will make them come a runnin'.
Easy and delicious.

4 thin (1/4-inch) veal cutlets
Salt and pepper
1 small egg, beaten with 1 teaspoon water
3/4 cup toasted bread crumbs
2 tablespoons vegetable oil
2 tablespoons butter
Wedges of lemon

Pound veal well to tenderize. Sprinkle with salt and pepper. Turn meat over in egg, then in crumbs; repeat. Heat oil and butter in heavy pan till bubbly, then sauté meat till brown on both sides. Drain on paper towels. Serve with lemon wedges. Serves 4.

NOTE: Try this with boneless chicken breasts—Panéed Poulet is divine! Panéed means breaded, but I used to think it meant you had to cook it in a pan—I never was too sure about those Cajun French words. My grandmother called the end of the French bread the "canoush." Don't try looking it up in a French dictionary. My nephew Keith says, "Cajun French bears no responsibility to correctness." He's got that right.

Longue Vue House and Gardens.

JAMBALAYA
(jum-bah-la-yah)

An African dish, ham (jamba) and rice (paella) are the main ingredients, but like gumbo, almost anything goes—right in the pot!

**1 pound smoked sausage, sliced (or ground)
1 large onion, chopped
1/2 bell pepper, chopped
2 cloves garlic, minced
1/2 pound ham chunks
1/2 teaspoon each: Salt, pepper, thyme
Worcestershire, soy sauce
1/8 teaspoon red pepper or more
2 1/2 cups water
1 cup uncooked rice
1 tablespoon chicken or beef bouillon granules
1 small can mushrooms, partially drained**

Brown sausage. Add onion, bell pepper, garlic, and ham, then spices. Stir till all are softened. Add water, rice, and bouillon. Bring to boil and stir well. Cover and cook over low heat 30 minutes; add mushrooms, stir, cover, and cook another 15 minutes. Serves 6 - 8.

NOTE: Jambalaya was traditionally made outdoors in huge black iron pots used for boiling sugar cane syrup, and was stirred with boat paddles. Since it can be made ahead, and with most any kind of meat, game, or seafood, it is a great dish for parties. For my son Shawn's rehearsal supper, we transported 10 gallon bags of it out of town along with salad makings, French Bread, and tins of cookies and tarts. We had fun decorating the hall and loved being able to entertain everybody who came from out of town, whether they were in the wedding party or not. The expense was minor, the enjoyment was major, and the toasts were roasts! Good food... memorable fun.

CREOLE OKRA
AND TOMATOES

Bring on the cornbread and iced tea!

1 large onion, chopped
1 - 2 tablespoons bacon grease
2 cups sliced okra
2 - 3 tablespoons flour
2 tomatoes, cut in chunks
1 teaspoon sugar
Salt and pepper to taste

Cook onion in bacon grease just for a minute on medium heat (go ahead and use vegetable oil, but understand that's not *real* Creole). Shake okra in flour and add to softened onion, cooking till okra is slightly browned (4 - 5 minutes). Add tomato chunks (canned is okay), sugar, and seasoning. Cover and simmer about 25 minutes, stirring occasionally. When it's soft and mushy, it's ready! Serves 4.

NOTE: Okra came from Africa, and tomatoes from South America and they probably got married in New Orleans! What a happy union!

STUFFED MIRLITONS
(mel'-ah-tahnz)

Also called a vegetable pear, chayote, or christophene, this pale green vegetable is mildly sweet and ideal for stuffing.

4 large mirlitons (or yellow squash or eggplants)
4 tablespoons butter
2 tablespoons vegetable oil
2 onions, chopped
1/2 cup chopped green pepper
2 cloves garlic, minced
2 teaspoons N'Awlins Seasoning (or 1/2 teaspoon each:
Salt, pepper, thyme, and basil)
1 cup chopped ham (or 2 cups ham and no seafood)
1 cup chopped shrimp, crawfish, or crabmeat
1 cup breadcrumbs
3/4 cup grated Cheddar cheese (optional)

Boil mirlitons in water to cover till fork tender (40-60 minutes). Cut in half, remove seeds, and drain cut-side down on paper towels.

In butter and oil, sauté onions, green pepper, and garlic until soft. Leaving shells intact, scoop out pulp from mirlitons and add to sautéed vegetables. Stir and add seasoning, ham, and seafood. Cook over medium heat about 15 minutes, stirring often. Add breadcrumbs last; stir well while cooking an additional 5 minutes.

Fill shells, sprinkle with cheese (or breadcrumbs and butter dots) and bake in baking dish at 350° about 20 minutes, or until tops are browned. Serves 8. Freezable; thaw before baking.

NOTE: Instead of breadcrumbs, try a 5-inch hunk of French bread soaked in ice water, then squeezed. This is good either way, trust me... G O O D!

LUNDI RED BEANS AND RICE

When it's Monday in New Orleans, it's time for red beans and rice. So good, and good for you....

1 pound dry red beans
8 cups water
1 meaty ham bone or 2 ham hocks
2 onions, chopped
2 cloves garlic, minced
2 bay leaves
Few shakes Tabasco sauce
Salt and pepper to taste

Place all in a big heavy pot. When it comes to a boil, lower and let it simmer, stirring occasionally, for at least three hours, but longer is fine. When they are soft enough, mash some of the beans against the side of the pot—makes for a wonderfully creamy sauce to serve over hot fluffy rice. Serves 6 - 8.

NOTE: Soaking the beans overnight cuts the cooking time in half. The seasoning meat varies: My Aunt Tiel wouldn't dream of making red beans without pickled pork, Ma Mère insisted on ham hocks, and my daddy liked hot sausage in his. But the real New Orleans secret is the ham bone marrow. Crack the bone to release that wonderful full-bodied flavor and creamy texture. A tradition that is still alive and well today, red beans and rice has always been cooked on Monday with the bone leftover from Sunday's ham. Before washing machines, that fit in quite well with the all-day chore of Monday washing. (Lundi is French for Monday; Mardi is Tuesday—bet you knew that.)

Courtyards and markets... a haven for strollers and shoppers.

BAKED CUSHAW

A big green and white crooked-neck squash—sweet and lov-er-ly

1 small cushaw (or small pumpkin)
3/4 cup butter
1 cup sugar
3/4 cup brown sugar
1/2 cup milk
4 eggs
1/2 teaspoon allspice
1/2 teaspoon nutmeg

Cut cleaned cushaw in half; remove seeds and fiber. Cut into pieces about 5 inches square. Boil in water to cover till tender; drain and scoop out shells. Mash pulp well in bowl with other ingredients. Fill 2 (8- or 9-inch) casserole dishes with mixture. Dot with butter and bake about 30 minutes at 350° till lightly browned. Each dish serves 6 or 8.

NOTE: These can be prepared ahead and refrigerated or frozen before baking. Adds a touch of sweetness—so pretty on the plate with an entrée and a green vegetable.

CANDIED YAMS

*Sweet potatoes are a New Orleans staple. I think this recipe
has been around as long as sugar... sugar at suppertime!*

**3 large sweet potatoes
2/3 cup brown or white sugar
1/4 cup butter or margarine
2 tablespoons water
1/2 teaspoon vanilla**

Parboil potatoes in jackets till barely soft. When cool,
peel and cut in fat (3/4 - inch) slices. Boil sugar, butter, water, and vanilla in skillet; add potatoes. Cover
and cook over low heat about 20 minutes, stirring gently a time or two. Uncover and cook another 10 minutes or so till thick and candied. Serves 4 - 6.

MAMAW'S EGGPLANT CASSEROLE

**1 eggplant, peeled and cubed
4 strips bacon (or ham), cut in pieces
1/2 onion, chopped
10 crackers (or *Frenchies*)
1/3 cup cream
3 tablespoons butter, divided
1/2 teaspoon each: Salt, lemon pepper, sugar
Buttered bread crumbs**

Soak eggplant in salt water about 20 minutes. Fry
bacon (or ham pieces) in large skillet till nearly done;
add chopped onion. Meanwhile soak crackers in
cream. Drain eggplant. Now add all to skillet. Cook
over low heat about 20 minutes, stirring often.

Place in buttered casserole dish and sprinkle buttered bread crumbs on top. Bake in 375° oven 15 minutes before serving. Serves 6.

NOTE: Mamaw also made this with shrimp—delish!

There's always fresh produce at the French Market.

MAQUE CHOU

(mock shoo)

A wonderful Indian dish of stewed corn and tomatoes.

**10 ears fresh corn (or 4 cups frozen or
canned whole kernal)
1 onion, chopped
2 tablespoons chopped bell pepper
1 clove garlic, minced
6 tablespoons butter
2 peeled, chopped tomatoes
1 teaspoon *N'Awlins Seasoning*
1 teaspoon sugar**

Scrape corn from cob saving all juice. Sauté onion, pepper and garlic in butter (or bacon fat). Add corn, tomatoes, seasoning and sugar. Stir and simmer over low heat about 40 minutes. Serves 6.

NOTE: The Creoles added a cup or so of cooked shrimp or crawfish to this dish and came up with a Creole rendition of an Indian dish.

SENSATION
SALAD DRESSING

Sensational, no other word for it.

4 ounces Romano cheese, grated
2 tablespoons bleu cheese, grated
2 cloves garlic, minced finely
3 tablespoons fresh lemon juice
1/3 cup olive oil
2/3 cup vegetable oil
1/2 teaspoon salt
1/4 teaspoon black pepper

Mix all together in a quart jar. Refrigerate.

Just before serving, stir well. For 4 servings, spoon about 3 tablespoons over 1/2 head of washed, torn and crisped lettuce with plenty of fresh parsley sprinkled on top. Toss lightly but thoroughly to coat.

NOTE: This dressing likes to be tossed lightly, never poured heavily. I don't recommend spooning it over individual salads. No need for a lot of salad vegetables—tossed with assorted crisp salad greens and parsley is just right!

MARIE'S
GARLIC TOMATO
MARINADE

1/3 cup onion, finely minced
5 baby toes garlic, finely minced
5 juicy tomatoes, chopped very small (save all juices)
1/2 teaspoon Creole seasoning
1 (8-ounce) bottle Wishbone Italian Dressing (or similar)
Salt and pepper to taste

Combine all in a serving bowl, being sure to get all the juice from the tomatoes. Refrigerate an hour or more.

At serving time, put the bowl on the table along with a big bowl of crisp lettuce and let everybody serve themselves. Mama Mia, that's *I-tah-yun*!

PECAN PIE
(peh-kauhn' pie)

If you insist on pronouncing it "pee-can," you're not allowed to make this.

3/4 cup sugar
3/4 cup light corn syrup
1 tablespoon flour
4 tablespoons butter or margarine, melted*
3 eggs
1 tablespoon vanilla
1 cup pecans
1 pie shell, unbaked

With whisk or fork, mix first 7 ingredients in order listed. Pour into pie shell and bake in preheated 350° oven about 45 minutes.

NOTE: For a delicious roasted pecan flavor, try browning the butter lightly in a skillet.

GWEN'S FLAKY PIE CRUST
1 cup flour
1/3 cup butter-flavored shortening
1/4 teaspoon salt
3 tablespoons ice water

Mix flour, shortening, and salt well with fork or pastry blender till mealy. Add water all at once and mix only till it holds together. Roll in circular shape on heavily floured cloth or board. Transfer to pie plate. Flute edges and prick bottom several times with fork. If baked shell is called for, bake in preheated 450° oven about 10 minutes until gently browned.

NOTE: If you want this to be flaky and divine, do not knead the dough—don't even think about it!

GRAMMY'S STRAWBERRY GLAZE PIE

There is no more delicious recipe for strawberry pie... and that's that!

2 pints fresh strawberries, washed and stemmed
1/2 cup water
1 cup sugar
3 tablespoons cornstarch
1 tablespoon butter
Red food coloring
1 baked pie shell
1/2 pint heavy cream, whipped with 1 tablespoon sugar

Put aside 8 small whole berries for garnish.

Take a handful of berries and squeeze enough into a small saucepan to make 1/2 cup. Leave rest of berries whole or halved. Combine sugar, cornstarch, and water with crushed berries. Bring to boil over medium heat and cook while stirring over low heat for 3 minutes, or until clear and thickened. Add a drop of red food coloring and butter. Stir and let cool.

Place berries into cooked pie shell and cover with cooled sauce. Top with real whipped cream and garnish with a few small whole berries. Refrigerate until ready to serve.

NOTE: Unlike the hollow-centered, lighter-colored berries grown elsewhere, South Louisiana strawberries are generally smaller, but firm all the way through—deep red, and sweet, sweet, sweet. Delicious in a waffle sauce or dessert glaze, they can also transform an ordinary bowl of cereal into an exciting dish! Buy them in the early spring in the French Market and enjoy eating them right out of the carton while you stroll around. Where y'at? Dawlin', you are *in* New Orleans!

*The St. Charles Avenue streetcar, one of the few remaining
electric trolley lines operating in the United States.*

CHOCOLATE ÉCLAIRS

1 cup water
1 stick butter or margarine
1 cup flour
1/4 teaspoon salt
4 large eggs
1 (small) box vanilla pudding (regular or instant)
2 cups cold milk
Chocolate Topping

Boil water in heavy pot; add butter and stir till melted. Add flour and salt all at once, stirring and cooking a minute or so till mixture forms soft ball that does not separate. Remove from heat, cool 10 minutes and add eggs one at a time, beating vigorously after each.

Form 12 - 15 spoonsful batter into smooth capsule shapes on a greased cookie sheet. Bake in 450° oven 15 minutes, then lower to 325° and bake another 25 minutes. While éclairs are baking, prepare and refrigerate pudding (package directions) and *Chocolate Topping*.

When éclairs are cool, slice top third off with sharp knife. Fill each éclair with about 2 tablespoons pudding. Replace top. Frost with *Chocolate Topping*. Refrigerate loosely covered (with sheet of waxed paper).

CHOCOLATE TOPPING: Melt 2 (1-ounce) squares unsweetened baking chocolate in micro on HIGH for 2 minutes (or over hot water on stovetop). Add 3 tablespoons butter; stir to melt. Add 1 1/4 cups powdered sugar, 1 teaspoon vanilla, and 2 - 3 tablespoons milk for thin consistency. Beat with spoon till glossy.

NOTE: Easier than you imagined, I'll bet. Cream Puffs are similar, but round, and sprinkled with powdered sugar. Try chocolate or lemon filling or stiffly whipped cream. I like cooked cream filling, but nobody complains when I use instant. (Yeah!) Use a large box to make 24 small puffs. This is my husband's favorite dessert. He says there's only one thing wrong with éclairs—I don't make them often enough.

MICROWAVE BREAD PUDDING

It's low calorie...and doesn't last long!

4-5 slices stale wheat bread
2 cups skim milk
3-4 tablespoons low-fat margarine
2/3 cup sugar (or 12 packets (1/4 cup) Sweet-N-Low)
3 eggs, slightly beaten (or egg substitute equivalent)
1 teaspoon vanilla
1/2 teaspoon cinnamon
1/2 cup raisins

In microwave baking dish (preferably a ring, but okay to use regular dish; just stir center to outside twice during baking), soak torn bread in milk. Melt margarine in 4-cup glass measure; add remaining ingredients to it. Pour over soaked bread, stirring only to distribute raisins. Microwave on ROAST (#7) for 11-12 minutes, until toothpick comes out clean.

NOTE: Bread Pudding is probably the most popular dessert in New Orleans—it is almost always on the menu. (I've been known to grab a go-cup at Messina's while strolling through the Quarter...Yum!)

If you make bread pudding in the morning for a later dessert, hide it—my boys did so much snitching, I decided to serve it intentionally for breakfast. They didn't mind at all. Sorry, but fresh bread simply does not work for bread pudding; it's too gummy. Coming up with stale bread has never been a problem for me. I managed to overheat the French rolls (again!) at our first cousin reunion, so I used my brick rolls to make bread pudding for breakfast the next morning. With fresh fruit and juice, it was much enjoyed, and cousins went home with a new breakfast idea.

NEW ORLEANS
BREAD PUDDING

1/2 loaf stale French bread
1 1/4 cups milk
1/3 stick butter
1/4 cup sugar
2 eggs
1 tablespoon vanilla
1/2 cup raisins

Soak stale French bread cubes in milk. Melt butter and add sugar, eggs, vanilla, and raisins. Mix all together with hands. Bake in buttered 8-inch baking pan about 45 minutes in 350° oven. If desired, serve with *Hard Sauce* and a dollop of whipped cream. Serves 6.

HARD SAUCE

4 tablespoons butter, room temperature
3 tablespoons sugar
1 teaspoon vanilla
2 tablespoons brandy, bourbon, or rum

Beat with beater or whisk till creamy and smooth.

NOTE: There are several other toppings for bread pudding. Custard sauce has an egg in it and is cooked a bit, but I don't make it cause mine likes to curdle and usually ends up looking like Egg Drop Soup. There's also meringue. And whipped cream. And if you spread strawberry preserves on top, it's called Queen's Pudding. One of my mother's favorite toppings is Lemon Sauce, which she makes with powdered sugar, lots of lemon juice, and "ah lil bud-ah."

BANANAS FOSTER

Dim the lights, delight your guests.

6 tablespoons butter
4 tablespoons brown sugar
4 ripe bananas, peeled and sliced lengthwise
1/2 teaspoon cinnamon
1/2 cup banana liqueur
1 cup white rum
4 large scoops vanilla ice cream

Melt butter in chafing dish or large skillet. Add brown sugar and blend. Add bananas and sauté. Sprinkle with cinnamon. Now pour the banana liqueur and the rum over the bananas and ignite, basting with the flaming liquid. Serve over ice cream when flame has died. Serves 4.

NOTE: New Orleans chefs love to flambé things like Crêpes Suzette, Cherries Jubilee, and Sweet Potato Brulé. The original recipe for *Bananas Foster* was created for one of Brennan's regular patrons named Richard Foster—it is recognized today as the crowning glory to an incomparable "Breakfast at Brennan's."

"How's it look?" Open-air markets offer a variety of goods.

MARDI GRAS KING CAKE
A tradition that's fun... and delicious!

1/2 cup milk
1/2 cup sugar
1 teaspoon salt
1/2 cup shortening
2 packages yeast
1/3 cup warm water
3 eggs
1 teaspoon grated lemon rind
1/2 teaspoon nutmeg
4 1/2 - 5 cups bread flour, sifted
1 tiny plastic baby, or a raw bean, or a pecan half
Lemon Glaze
Colored sugar

Combine milk, sugar, salt and shortening in saucepan. Scald, then cool to lukewarm. Dissolve yeast in warm water in large bowl, then add eggs, lemon rind, nutmeg, milk mixture, and 2 cups flour; beat till smooth. Add remaining flour a cup at a time. Knead on floured board till smooth and elastic. Place in greased bowl, turn, then cover with damp cloth. Let rise in warm place about 2 hours.

Punch dough down and knead again about 5 minutes. Divide into thirds and roll each into a strip about 30 inches long. Braid strips and place on greased baking sheet, pressing ends together to form oval. Now insert baby or bean into dough. Cover and let rise until double, about an hour.

Bake in preheated 375° oven about 20 minutes till golden brown. Cool and frost, then immediately sprinkle sugar stripes of purple, green and yellow around the ring (easy to put 1/3 cup sugar with a little food coloring in a food processor to get even color; blend red and blue to make purple). Decorate with halved candied cherries if desired. Freezable... and fun!

LEMON GLAZE

1 1/2 cups powdered sugar
2 tablespoons lemon juice
1 tablespoon water

Combine all and stir till smooth, adding more water if necessary to make easily spreadable so that it will slowly drip down the sides of the cake.

NOTE: King Cakes celebrate the finding of baby Jesus on the Epiphany, January 6th, by the Three Wise Men. The lucky person who finds the baby in the cake is declared King or Queen for the day... and is obliged to bring a King Cake to the next seasonal celebration. Traditionally King Cakes are oval-shaped to show unity of all Christians, and are the Mardi Gras colors of purple, yellow, and green. Mardi Gras means Fat Tuesday and marks the beginning of Lent—and the end of King Cakes.

CREAMY PRALINES
(praw-leenz)

I am proud to share this outstanding McKee family recipe that has been handed down by word of mouth. Here are clear instructions to let you in on the secret.

2 cups sugar
1 cup buttermilk
1 teaspoon baking soda
1 stick butter or margarine
1 teaspoon vanilla
1 - 1 1/2 cups shelled pecan halves

Prepare for pralines by stretching two 3-foot pieces of waxed paper over 2 sheets of newspaper on a countertop or table (the wax may transfer to the counter unless you buffer it with newspaper). Run the stick of butter you will use in the recipe over the waxed paper.

Put first 3 ingredients in large heavy Dutch oven and bring to a boil stirring constantly. Have last 3 ingredients ready beside pot. Lower heat slightly when mixture rises to top of pot, and stir, watching the white bubble up and change to yellow, then beige, then it goes down and gets light brown. When it begins to thicken slightly (all this takes about 7 minutes), drip a few drops into a cup of cold water. When your fingers can make a little ball of the drops, carefully add the last 3 ingredients—it may spatter because it is so hot, but stirring tames it. Stir and heat about another minute till drops test to softball in the water again—this is very important to let it come to this stage again. Now remove it from the heat and let it sit there for one minute, no more, while you rest your stirring arm.

Now stir like mad with wooden spoon for just a couple of minutes till you can feel the mixture becoming a little thick. This is where you must decide you are in control of the situation! You don't want to dip it while it is still runny, nor do you want it to get so thick that it hardens in the pot. Tilt the pot so that you can dip spoonfuls onto the waxed paper from the sides of the pot where it hardens more quickly. Allow to harden. (Don't try to be too neat—drips can be consumed immediately!)

NOTE: My sister Janet's Christmas dinner is yearly proclaimed to be "the best ever." I arrived one year to find her quite distressed because her pralines never did harden. We scraped them up with a spatula, put them back into the pot, heated to the softball stage, stirred, and dipped. Voila! Perfect!

Mardi Gras. "Hey, mis-tah, throw me somethin!"

HURRICANE PUNCH

"Walkin' in New Orleans" usually includes a stroll down Bourbon Street. The sights, sounds, and smells are unequaled anywhere. There's always a crowd at St. Peter Street, probably going to or coming from Pat O'Brien's, where this tasty tall one was made famous. Suitably named for the turbulent storms that come swirling in from the Gulf, its lovely cherry-red color gives the hurricane glass a cheery glow. (Be forewarned, the glass is not the only thing that it puts a glow on.)

Crushed ice
2 ounces Jero's Red Passion Fruit Cocktail Mix
(any passion fruit juice will work)
2 ounces fresh lemon juice
4 ounces good dark rum per glass
1 orange slice
1 maraschino cherry

Fill a hurricane glass (any 16-ounce glass will do—it just won't look as enticing) with crushed ice; add cocktail mix, lemon juice, and rum. Decorate with orange slice and cherry.

NOTE: There's a Pat O'Brien's Hurricane Mix, too (and their Bloody Mary Mix is wow!). If you can't find it or Jero's for your Night in New Orleans party, mix a 48-ounce can Hawaiian Punch with a 12-ounce can frozen orange juice and a 6-ounce can frozen lemonade, then pour this over the crushed ice and rum.

So many tourists buy a Hurricane for the glass, that it is assumed you want to do so, and you pay for the glass when you buy the drink. Of course you can turn it in and get your deposit back, but somebody in your group always wants the glass. You can also get a Cyclone, a Squall, a Breeze . . . each has its own glass, is pretty, colorful . . . and stormy.

MILK PUNCH

Lovely before brunch... or after the ball.

1 jigger brandy or bourbon
4 ounces light cream
1 teaspoon powdered sugar
1/2 teaspoon vanilla
Cracked ice (4 cubes)
Sprinkle of nutmeg

In a cocktail shaker (or blender), mix all but nutmeg. Shake a lot! Shake some more. Serve in a pretty glass with a sprinkle of nutmeg. Serves 1.

NOTE: These and others such as a Ramos Gin Fizz, a Sazerac Cocktail, and an Absinthe Frappé, have been famous New Orleans drinks for years. New ones are concocted every day, like a Hand Grenade, a Horney Gator, Voodoo Beer.... Hmmm.... No wonder New Orleans is the city that care forgot.

CAFÉ BRULOT
(cah-fay broo-low)

The flaming is entertaining; the taste, devilishly delicious!

**Peel of one orange
2 cinnamon sticks
8 whole cloves
2 tablespoons sugar
3 ounces Cognac
3 cups hot strong black coffee**

Heat all but the coffee in a fireproof bowl or chafing dish. When hot, but not boiling, bring to table and ignite with a match. Ladle and stir a couple of minutes, then pour the hot coffee into the flaming brandy. Ladle into brulot or demitasse cups.

NOTE: Many of the famous drinks in New Orleans have their own containers. Antoine's, the father of this one, uses a special copper Brulot bowl and Café Brulot cups. **Café Diable** has lemon peel instead of orange, and sometimes Cointreau. Ideally, this is meant to warm the inside of the body, so if you don't want to flambé your arm along with the café, you might try filling a long metal spoon with the brandy and lighting the match under it, then ignite the bowl.

Shadows fall on the statue of Andrew Jackson.
Jackson Square.

ABOUT THE AUTHOR

Gwen McKee, a native Louisianian, has had the good fortune to enjoy New Orleans cooking all her life. Born and raised in Baton Rouge, Gwen considered "going to New Orleans" the ultimate treat, always a wonderful eating experience whether it was in the home of her grandmother or an aunt or cousin, or dining out. She has written *The Little Gumbo Book* and edited *Best of the Best from Louisiana*, two of the most popular cookbooks in Louisiana. As director of her own publishing company (Quail Ridge Press), she personally edits all cookbooks, both editorially and "tastefully" in her favorite office—the kitchen.

Other Louisiana Favorites

The Little Gumbo Book $8.95

Best of the Best from Louisiana Cookbook..........$16.95

Best of the Best from Louisiana Cookbook II $16.95

Recipe Hall of Fame Collection

The extensive recipe database of Quail Ridge Press' acclaimed BEST OF THE BEST STATE COOKBOOK SERIES is the inspiration behind the RECIPE HALL OF FAME COLLECTION. These Hall-of-Fame recipes have achieved extra distinction for consistently producing superb dishes. Appetizers to desserts, quick dishes to masterpiece presentations, the RECIPE HALL OF FAME COLLECTION has it all.

The Recipe Hall of Fame Cookbook $19.95

The Recipe Hall of Fame Cookbook II $19.95

Recipe Hall of Fame Quick & Easy Cookbook $19.95

Recipe Hall of Fame Dessert Cookbook $16.95

NOTE: All four Hall of Fame cookbooks can be ordered as a set for $53.95 (plus shipping), a 30% discount off the total list price of $76.80.

To order using a credit card call 1-800-343-1583 or visit our website at www.quailridge.com.

To order by mail, please add $4.00 postage for any number of books ordered and send check or money order to:

ⓠ QUAIL RIDGE PRESS
P. O. Box 123 • Brandon, MS 39043

Mississippi residents add 7% sales tax.
Books may also be available at book stores and gift shops.

For more information or a free catalog featuring the 41-volume BEST OF THE BEST STATE COOKBOOK SERIES, call 1-800-343-1583 or visit us on the web at www.quailridge.com.